*With Love*

*and*

*Peace*

## Acknowledgments

*To all my friends and family who willingly gave of their time to edit the stories of my twelve books; patiently taught me computer jargon; shared their computer skills with I-design and Photoshop; and guided me through the copyright, ISBN and barcode maze. I couldn't have done it without you.*

# The Graduation
# Study Guide

Original copyrights © from 1997 to 2011

ISBN: 978-1-947573-12-3

Library of Congress Catalog number: 2017912137

The Carolee Collectables
Printed in the United States of America
www.crystalsforkids.org

*Carolee O'Neill*
http://books2c4kids.com

Chocolate

Book has been handcrafted from cover to cover,
including the watercolor illustrations by Carolee.

Study Guide Questions for Chapter One

1.  Mention some things Annie's parents could have done to make the transition to the academy easier.

    _____

    _____

    _____

    _____

2.  Would they be things you would want done for you? Explain.

    _____

    _____

    _____

    _____

3.  What were her parents' reasons for sending her to the academy?

    _____

    _____

    _____

    _____

4.  Did Annie know what a "finishing school" was and what that meant to her? Explain what it means to you.

    _____

    _____

    _____

    _____

5.  Were Annie's feelings considered in this first chapter? State why you think they were or were not.

    _____

    _____

    _____

    _____

6. What was Annie's impression of the sister who took her to the dorm?

_____

_____

_____

7. How would you have felt under these circumstances?

_____

_____

_____

# The Graduation Study Guide

## Study Guide Questions for Chapter Two

1. State if you feel Annie's anger was justified when she was confronted with all the rules for the dorm. Explain why you feel this way?

   _____

   _____

   _____

2. What did Annie's background have to do with why she was sent to the academy?

   _____

   _____

   _____

3. Had Annie's siblings been sent for private schooling? If so, why did Annie react the way she did? Explain.

   _____

   _____

   _____

4. Would Annie's reaction to the rules and to being sent away be seen as normal for a thirteen year old by her parents? Please explain if you think Annie over-reacted to her situation.

   _____

   _____

   _____

5. Explain how Annie reacted to being surrounded by girls. In spite of this, did she make friends easily? Give examples.

   _____

   _____

   _____

6. Explain how Annie was reacting to the rules and discipline of the dorm and the school.

   _____

   _____

   _____

   _____

7. After learning that many of the girls at the academy had been abandoned by their families, how did Annie identify with them? Explain why you think she felt this way.

   _____

   _____

   _____

   _____

# The Graduation Study Guide

## Study Guide for Chapter Three

1. What was Annie's impression of Sister Mary Florentine?

   _____
   _____
   _____
   _____

2. How did Lucy react to Sister? Explain why she felt like that. How did you feel about her

   _____
   _____
   _____
   _____

3. Do you have any teachers to compare Sister Mary Florentine with or a principal? Explain why.

   _____
   _____
   _____
   _____

4. The girls had just been introduced to a set of rules for the dorm. On top of those they were told about the demerit cards. Explain this system and what you thought about it.

   _____
   _____
   _____
   _____

5. At the age of thirteen was it possible for Annie to have valid feelings toward her friends? Explain your reasons for your answer.

   _____
   _____
   _____
   _____

6.  At what age would you like your parents to understand that your feelings for your friends can be serious? How would you feel if you were a parent? What about the opposite sex?

    _____
    _____
    _____
    _____

7.  Were Annie's parents considerate of her feelings? Explain your answer.

    _____
    _____
    _____
    _____

# The Graduation Study Guide

Study Guide for Chapter Four

1.  Was this a different lifestyle for Annie than she
    was used to? Explain.

    _____

    _____

    _____

    _____

2.  Were all of the girls Catholic? If not, name one.
    Why would parents put a girl who was not of
    this religion into this academy?

    _____

    _____

    _____

    _____

3.  Were there any girls you or your parents would
    consider hard-core? If so, name one.

    _____

    _____

    _____

    _____

4.  Did Annie have a negative experience with a
    nun as a little girl? State what effect this could
    have had on how Annie responded to her new
    environment.

    _____

    _____

    _____

    _____

5.  What kind of a relationship did Annie have with
    the boarding students? Explain.

    _____

    _____

    _____

    _____

6. Was Annie a fun loving girl but basically
   honest? Name an incident that makes you say so.

   _____

   _____

   _____

   _____

7. Was the comradeship shared between the girls a
   way to cope with their situation? Explain your
   answer.

   _____

   _____

   _____

   _____

# The Graduation Study Guide

## Study Guide Questions for Chapter Five

1.  Did Annie's father's reassurances allow her to come to accept the academy? If no, was there something else he or her mother could have done?

    _____
    _____
    _____
    _____

2.  At this point did Annie feel her father cared?

    _____
    _____
    _____
    _____

3.  Assuming Annie loved her dad, would this have made the situation more difficult for her to understand? Explain.

    _____
    _____
    _____
    _____

4.  How did the girls on the bleachers respond to Annie being at the game? Do you feel they were justified in their actions? Explain. How would you have felt about this?

    _____
    _____
    _____
    _____

5.  What sort of a girl do you think Annie was? Did she care about her friends at the academy? Did they trust her? Give examples.

    _____
    _____

_____

_____

6. Was Annie a difficult young woman for her
   parents to manage or did she generally follow
   the rules? Give an example.

   _____

   _____

   _____

7. Was Annie a leader or a follower? State why
   you think so.

   _____

   _____

   _____

   _____

# The Graduation Study Guide

Study Guide Question for Chapter Six

1. Was Sister Mary Margaret fair with the girls when she caught them in the middle of their antics?

   _____

   _____

   _____

2. Was Sister's response a form of discipline? Explain what you think she did and why.

   _____

   _____

   _____

3. Were Annie's parents impressed with Michael? Why or why not? Would you have been impressed with him if you were Annie's sister?

   _____

   _____

   _____

4. What was your reaction to how Annie was treated by Shirley? by Mr. Kelley?

   _____

   _____

   _____

5. What was the bond of honesty Annie was expected to live up to within the family unit? State what it was.

   _____

   _____

   _____

   _____

Carolee O'Neill

6. What was Betsy's relationship with Annie?
   Explain how this could be of help to Annie at
   this time in her life.

   _____

   _____

   _____

   _____

7. Were Annie's parents fair when it came to
   listening to Michael and her side of the story?
   Explain.

   _____

   _____

   _____

   _____

# The Graduation Study Guide

## Study Guide Questions for Chapter Seven

1. Do you feel Annie's punishment was justified? Could there been a different solution?

   _____

   _____

   _____

2. When Annie first heard about Michael's illness, was her reaction responsible? Explain why you think she felt this way. Did she care deeply about him? Explain.

   _____

   _____

   _____

3. What did Annie's uncertainty in her life have to do with her reaction to Michael's illness?

   _____

   _____

   _____

4. How did Annie feel about going to the chapel with Sister Eunice? Explain how you would have felt under these conditions.

   _____

   _____

   _____

5. Did Annie believe in God? Give reasons that support your answer.

   _____

   _____

   _____

   _____

6. Was Michael's illness a difficult experience for Annie? Was it a loss to her emotionally? How did it compare with the loss of her other friends. Explain your answers with examples.

_____
_____
_____
_____

7. Do traumatic events bring people closer together or separate them? Explain how and why.

_____
_____
_____
_____

# The Graduation Study Guide

## Study Guide Questions for Chapter Eight

1. Explain how Annie directed her anger after having to deal with Michael's situation and being campused.

   _____

   _____

   _____

2. Was Annie respectful of her father? Give an example that supports your answer.

   _____

   _____

   _____

3. Was Annie careless in her date selection for the Sadie Hawkins dance?

   _____

   _____

   _____

4. Explain how Annie's naivety or carelessness manifested itself in other situations.

   _____

   _____

   _____

5. Did Annie and Jerry come from the same type of backgrounds? Are similar backgrounds important? Explain.

   _____

   _____

   _____

6. Compare their backgrounds with what a teen deals with today. Are your friends generally

from similar backgrounds or are they diverse?
Explain the pros and cons of these differences.

_____

_____

_____

_____

7.  Was this part of the problem with Annie's
    relationship with Jerry? Give an example to
    support your answer.

_____

_____

_____

_____

# The Graduation Study Guide

## Study Guide Questions for Chapter Nine

1. Explain how you felt about all the rules for the dorm and the school. Did they maintain order or weren't they necessary? Explain your answer.

   _____

   _____

   _____

2. Was Annie on common ground with Betsy as a friend? eg: Did they come from similar backgrounds?

   _____

   _____

   _____

3. State how you think Annie behaved at the party. Was she comfortable with this class of people? Explain.

   _____

   _____

   _____

4. Annie had a pre-determined idea of why nuns went into the convent. What was it?

   _____

   _____

   _____

5. State if you felt Annie continued to hope Michael would recover. Were her hopes sincere or shallow? Explain.

   _____

   _____

   _____

6. Was Annie's reaction to seeing Michael in the store a responsible one? Did her reaction conflict with how she felt about him? Explain your answers.

_____

_____

_____

7. Did the nuns provide a consistent atmosphere so the girls knew what to expect? Explain if you feel this was a good or bad thing and why.

_____

_____

_____

_____

# The Graduation Study Guide

Study Questions for Chapter Ten

1.  Had Annie resolved her relationship with
    Michael before she met Tony? What could she
    have done about that, if anything?

    _____

    _____

    _____

2.  Was Annie vulnerable at this point in her life?
    Would this be a reason for Annie to turn to Jerry
    or Tony?

    _____

    _____

    _____

3.  Were her feelings for Michael and Tony
    genuine? State why you feel this and what you
    would have done under similar circumstances.

    _____

    _____

    _____

4.  Explain how you felt about the relationship
    between Annie and Tony. How did Annie cope
    with this as another possible loss for her?

    _____

    _____

    _____

5.  Did Annie show respect for Tony's vocation?
    Do you feel she did the right thing? If so, state
    why you think so.

    _____

    _____

_____

6. Did Annie have anyone to turn to when things got difficult? If so, state who they were.

_____

_____

_____

7. What role did Annie's grandparents play in her life? Had they taught her any valuable lessons?

_____

_____

_____

_____

# The Graduation Study Guide

## Study Guide Questions for Chapter Eleven

1.  Does Annie fall in love too easily, or would you consider her behavior normal for her age? Give reasons to support your answer.

    _____

    _____

    _____

    _____

2.  As Annie and Jerry were from different backgrounds, please address their value systems and if they were comparable.

    _____

    _____

    _____

    _____

3.  Was Annie caught between two different worlds? If you feel this is true, explain.

    _____

    _____

    _____

    _____

4.  As Annie's mother did not approve of Jerry, do you feel Annie's decision to continue to see him was a wise one? State the pros and cons of the relationship.

    _____

    _____

    _____

    _____

5.  In this chapter we find that Lucie would no longer be a boarding student. How did this affect Annie?

    _____

    _____

_____

6. As Annie walked along the school grounds close
   to St. Joseph's, do you feel that deep down
   inside Annie knew she would never see Tony
   again? Would you have felt this way?

   _____
   _____
   _____

7. Compare your relationship with your friends to
   Annie's relationships with Grace and Lucie. Are
   they the same or different?

   _____
   _____
   _____
   _____

# The Graduation Study Guide

Study Guide Questions for Chapter Twelve

1. What are the possibilities that Annie's earlier idea of how nuns got into the convent had something to do with Sister Claudia's attitude and personality?

_____
_____

2. Had Annie been treated fairly by most of the nuns? Name some. Had these nuns taught her some valuable lessons through discipline and consistency?

_____
_____

3. Explain your reaction to Annie getting locked out on the balcony by Sister Claudia? Did she deserve this? Explain your answer. How did the boarding students feel about this?

_____
_____
_____

4. How did you feel about the scene on Thanksgiving Day? Was Annie justified with her actions? Explain. Name two things she was trying to accomplish.

_____
_____
_____

5. Can you say what Jerry's main focus was when it came to Annie and girls on the whole? Did Jerry's behavior show signs of his intent Annie should have recognized? Name them.

23.

_____
_____
_____
_____

6. Did Annie's parents and siblings believe her explanations? Did anyone try to follow up on Annie's concerns? Explain your responses.

_____
_____
_____
_____

7. Was Annie treated in a hurtful way when her grandfather died?
Explain. Was Annie compassionate toward her grandmother's situation? Explain.

_____
_____
_____
_____

# The Graduation Study Guide

## Study Guide Questions for Chapter Thirteen

1.  How do you feel Annie's father responded to the accident with his new car? Had Jerry acted responsibly? Explain your answers.

    _____

    _____

    _____

2.  How did the accident affect Annie's relationship with her older sister, if at all?

    _____

    _____

    _____

3.  What was Annie's main outlet that kept her focused during her academy years? Was it a form of discipline? Explain how it could be. What about its use in the future?

    _____

    _____

    _____

4.  How did you feel about the revenge Jeannie and Annie took against Sister Claudia? Do you feel this was right? State your pros and cons. What else could they have done?

    _____

    _____

    _____

5.  Should Annie have gone to the chapel to pray about some of the things that were happening? Should she have turned them over to God? What would you have done?

    _____

_____
_____
_____

6. Was Annie an easy young woman for her
   parents to manage? Is she the sort of girl you
   would like as a friend? Was she trustworthy and
   fair to her friends? Explain your answers.

_____
_____
_____
_____

7. Did Annie generally associate with the right
   crowd at the academy? At home? Give
   examples.

_____
_____
_____
_____

# The Graduation Study Guide

Study Guide Questions for Chapter Fourteen

1. Did Annie use common sense, staying with Jerry? Explain your answer. When he joined the service, was she fearful of another loss? Discuss. Why was he running away?

_____

_____

_____

2. Did you feel Annie's brother, Chuck, did everything he could? Why didn't he overrule his grandmother and stop Annie?

_____

_____

_____

3. Did Annie finally realize too late that she was as naïve as Chuck said she was? Discuss.

_____

_____

_____

_____

4. Explain if you feel Jerry's actions were a form of date rape? Did he treat Annie fairly? Do you know anyone who has had this happen to her? Did Annie blame him or herself for what had happened? Discuss.

_____

_____

_____

_____

5. Explain how Annie tried to manage her problem alone, before turning to her friend, Betsy. How did that work? Would you have done anything differently?

_____

_____
_____
_____

6. Explain how you would have felt in Annie's shoes against Sister Edward. Although Sister had to consider the standing of the school, could her actions have been more considerate?

_____
_____
_____

7. Here we see a contrast between Sister Eunice and Sister Edward, different types of personalities. Are there similar differences in your life with teachers or friends? Explain.

_____
_____
_____

Study Guide Questions for Chapter Fifteen

1. Explain in your own words the trauma/losses Annie endured because of this pregnancy. Were they long lasting? Could Annie have become a bitter person because of it?

   _____

   _____

   _____

   _____

2. How did Annie respond to being expelled from the academy? Discuss your feelings.

   _____

   _____

   _____

3. Do you know young people who have suffered losses due to circumstances beyond their control? Discuss how they handled it and or how you handled it, if that's the case.

   _____

   _____

4. Jane was six years older than Annie. What would be reasons for why it took a traumatic event to bring them closer? Did Annie's journey offer examples of how to deal with others?

   _____

   _____

   _____

5. Compare the differences between Annie's father's reaction to her mother's on the pregnancy. Do you feel Annie's situation could have turned out differently with better communication? Discuss.

29.

_____
_____
_____
_____

6. Discuss how Annie's mother felt about the
   differences in Annie's and Jerry's backgrounds.
   Was Annie's mother's reaction the only way she
   could deal with her daughter's losses at the
   time? Discuss your answers and state why.

_____
_____
_____
_____

7. Was anyone aware of what was happening to
   Annie over this four year period? If so, who?
   Were people too busy to notice—are people too
   busy to notice today?

_____
_____
_____
_____

# The Graduation Study Guide

## Study Guide Questions for Chapter Sixteen

1.  What do you feel could have been done so Annie could have kept her scholarship, completed her recital and graduated?

    _____

    _____

    _____

2.  Not receiving absolution/forgiveness from the priest set what actions into motion? Was Annie trying to follow what she had been taught and do the right thing? Explain.

    _____

    _____

3.  Do you feel Jerry was sensitive to the losses Annie incurred? Due to the differences in backgrounds, was he able to understand these types of losses? Discuss this.

    _____

    _____

4.  Explain what you think Annie's mother said to Jerry's parents when they came to drop him off for the marriage with the justice of peace. Could it have been fact or fiction?

    _____

    _____

5.  After the marriage by the justice of the peace, Annie's father hoped the parish priest would marry them. If the marriage failed, an annulment could be obtained. Explain why? Was he trying to help them?

    _____

_____
_____
_____

6. Do you feel the rules were too strict? Are we
   lacking in strict rules today and a strong value
   system? Have any of your friends or family
   suffered due to situations with drugs or
   abortion?

_____
_____
_____
_____

7. How does Annie's story parallel a teen's life
   today? Share similarities and differences.

_____
_____
_____
_____

# The Graduation Study Guide

### Study Guide Questions for Chapter Seventeen

1. Why did Annie decide to leave home and join Jerry in Georgia? Was this a mature decision on her part? Discuss the pros and cons of this decision.

_____

_____

_____

_____

2. Are teens today equipped to make this kind of a decision at the age of seventeen?

_____

_____

_____

_____

3. Did the years of continuity and discipline at home and at the academy contribute to Annie's ability to make this decision? Explain your answer.

_____

_____

_____

_____

4. How do you think Annie's family felt about her leaving and going out into the world? How would your family have felt? Expound on this.

_____

_____

_____

_____

5. When we consider Annie's father, do you think he was caught between two women he loved? Discuss this possibility.

_____

_____

_____

6. Were Annie's parents aware of the possible pregnancy due to Annie being naïve? Should parents guide their families in these matters?

_____
_____
_____

7. How did Annie's relationship with her grandmother bring about a meaningful resolution for Annie in the end?

_____
_____
_____

8. Explain in your own words how the lessons Annie learned during these years could be of benefit to her later in life.

_____
_____
_____

9. State if you believe these lessons still are applicable in today's world for a teen and a family.

_____
_____
_____

10. Can you compare the differences and similarities of your family and Annie's?

_____
_____
_____

# The Graduation Study Guide

_____

_____

11. Does your family meet on a regular basis to
    discuss concerns?
    Do you feel this is an important part of growing
    up? If so, why do you think so? Have you shared
    these feelings with your parents and or family?

    _____

    _____

    _____

12. Concerning Jerry, had Annie played with fire
    and didn't realize it?  Did Jerry understand
    Annie's losses? Explain

    _____

    _____

    _____

13. Discuss the title used for the novel. What was its
    connection with the story? Why did the author
    chose it to describe the novel?

    _____

    _____

    _____

    _____

35.

Carolee O'Neill

# The Carolee Collectables

## by Carolee O'Neill

Goodie RudeShoes: Series One, children 5 to 100.
Billy BitterBetter: Series Two, children 5 to 100.
Granny NeatFreak: children 4 to 100.
The Mouse House:   children 4 to 100.
That Secret Part of Me: children 3 to 100.
From Silly to Sinister: Short Stories:
Book One and Two.
Fiction for teens through mature adults.
Navigating the Potholes of Life:
Fiction for teen and adult.
Adventure, comedy, drama.
A Reason to Dream:
Fiction for teen and adult.
Drama based on a true Story.
Three versions of The Graduation.
The Graduation: A stand-alone novel
for teens and adults.
The Graduation with Study Guide
for the parent with teens, teens and adults.
The Graduation Study Guide for
the person who prefers a separate copy of the guide.
Fiction: suspense, humor, insightful.
With God in Mind.
Thought provoking prose for
teens through mature adults.

caroleeagain1934@gmail.com
http://books2c4kids.com

Books are available as paperback and as ebooks.
Thank you for your interest in my work.

Carolee O'Neill

www.ingramcontent.com/pod-product-compliance
Lightning Source LLC
Chambersburg PA
CBHW060702280326
41933CB00012B/2273